EASY POP MELODIES
FOR CLARINET

ISBN 978-1-4803-8429-3

HAL•LEONARD®
CORPORATION

7777 W. BLUEMOUND RD. P.O. BOX 13819 MILWAUKEE, WI 53213

ALL MY LOVING

CLARINET

Words and Music by JOHN LENNON
and PAUL McCARTNEY

BEAUTY AND THE BEAST
from Walt Disney's BEAUTY AND THE BEAST

Clarinet

Lyrics by HOWARD ASHMAN
Music by ALAN MENKEN

BLOWIN' IN THE WIND

CLARINET

Words and Music by
BOB DYLAN

CAN YOU FEEL THE LOVE TONIGHT
from Walt Disney Pictures' THE LION KING

Clarinet

Music by ELTON JOHN
Lyrics by TIM RICE

CAN'T HELP FALLING IN LOVE

CLARINET

Words and Music by GEORGE DAVID WEISS,
HUGO PERETTI and LUIGI CREATORE

CLOCKS

Words and Music by GUY BERRYMAN,
JON BUCKLAND, WILL CHAMPION
and CHRIS MARTIN

CLARINET

DAYDREAM BELIEVER

CLARINET

Words and Music by
JOHN STEWART

DON'T KNOW WHY

CLARINET

Words and Music by
JESSE HARRIS

DON'T STOP BELIEVIN'

CLARINET

Words and Music by STEVE PERRY,
NEAL SCHON and JONATHAN CAIN

EDELWEISS
from THE SOUND OF MUSIC

Clarinet

Lyrics by OSCAR HAMMERSTEIN II
Music by RICHARD RODGERS

EIGHT DAYS A WEEK

CLARINET

Words and Music by JOHN LENNON
and PAUL McCARTNEY

Moderately fast

1., 3. Ooh, I need your love, babe; guess you know it's true.
2. Love you ev - 'ry day, girl; al - ways on my mind.

Hope you need my love, babe, just like I need you.
One thing I can say, babe, girl: love you all the time.

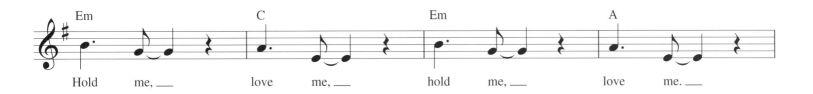

Hold me, ___ love me, ___ hold me, ___ love me. ___

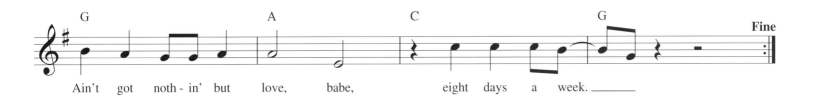

Ain't got noth - in' but love, babe, eight days a week. _____ **Fine**

Eight days a week I love _____ you.

Eight days a week is not e - nough to show I care. _ **D.C. al Fine**

EVERY BREATH YOU TAKE

CLARINET

Music and Lyrics by
STING

Moderately

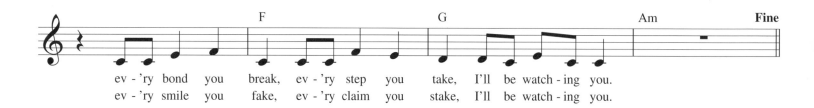

Ev -'ry breath you __ take, ev -'ry move you __ make,
Ev -'ry move you __ make, ev -'ry vow you __ break,

ev -'ry bond you break, ev -'ry step you take, I'll be watch - ing you.
ev -'ry smile you fake, ev -'ry claim you stake, I'll be watch - ing you.

Ev -'ry sin - gle __ day, ev -'ry word you __ say,

ev -'ry game you play, ev -'ry night you stay, I'll be watch-ing you.

Oh, can't you __ see you be - long to __ me?

How my poor heart __ aches __ with ev -'ry step __ you take.

FIREFLIES

CLARINET

Words and Music by
ADAM YOUNG

GEORGIA ON MY MIND

Clarinet

Words by STUART GORRELL
Music by HOAGY CARMICHAEL

IN MY LIFE

CLARINET

Words and Music by JOHN LENNON
and PAUL McCARTNEY

HEY, SOUL SISTER

CLARINET

Words and Music by PAT MONAHAN,
ESPEN LIND and AMUND BJORKLAND

Moderately

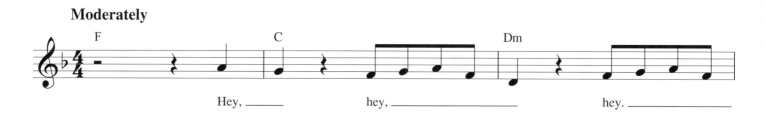

Hey, _____ hey, _____ hey. _____

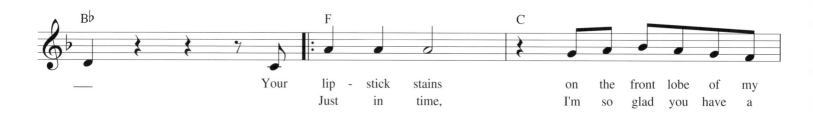

_____ Your lip - stick stains on the front lobe of my
Just in time, I'm so glad you have a

left - side brains. I know I wouldn't for - get ya, and so I went and
one - track mind like me. You gave my life di - rec - tion, a game show love con -

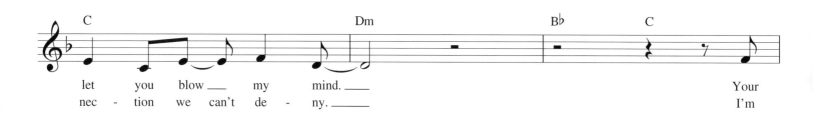

let you blow ___ my mind. ___ Your
nec - tion we can't de - ny. ___ I'm

sweet moon - beam, the smell of you in ev - 'ry sin - gle dream I dream.
so ob - sessed; my heart is bound to beat right out my un - trimmed chest. _

_____ I knew when we col - lid - ed you're the one I have de - cid - ed who's one of my kind. _
_____ I be - lieve in you; like a vir - gin, you're Ma - don - na, and I'm al - ways gon - na

wanna blow your mind.) Hey, soul sis - ter, ain't _

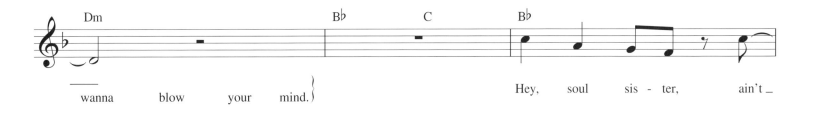

_____ that Mis - ter Mis - ter on the ra - di - o, ster - e - o? The way you move ain't fair, you know.

Hey, soul sis - ter, I _____ don't wan - na miss a sin - gle thing you do _____

_____ to - night. Hey, _____ hey, _____

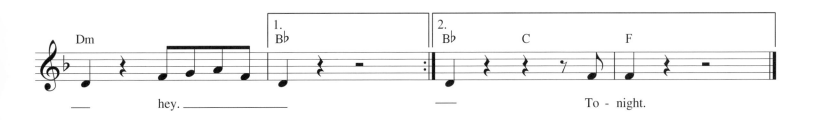

_____ hey. _____ To - night.

HOT N COLD

CLARINET

Words and Music by KATY PERRY,
MAX MARTIN and LUKASZ GOTTWALD

Moderately fast

You change your mind ____ like a girl ____ chang - es clothes. ____
We used to be ____ just like twins, ____ so in sync. ____

____ Yeah, you P - M - S ____ like a girl; ____
____ The same en - er - gy ____ now's a dead

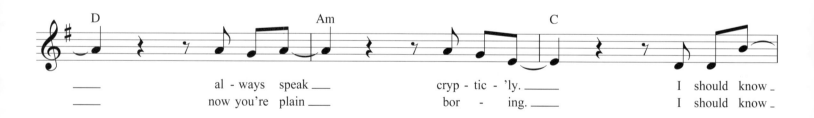

____ I would know. ____ And you o - ver - think, ____
____ bat - ter - y. ____ Used to laugh 'bout noth - ing; ____

al - ways speak ____ cryp - tic - 'ly. ____ I should know ____
now you're plain ____ bor - ing. ____ I should know ____

____ that you're ____ no good ____ for me. ____
____ that you're ____ not gon - na change. ____

'Cause you're hot ___ then you're cold. You're yes ___ then you're no. You're in ___

___ then you're out. You're up ___ then you're down. You're wrong ___ when it's right. It's black ___

___ and it's white. We fight, ___ we break up. We kiss, ___ we make up. ___

You don't real - ly wan - na stay, no, ___ but you don't real - ly wan - na

go. ___ You're hot ___ then you're cold. You're yes ___ then you're no. You're in ___

___ then you're out. You're up ___ then you're down. ___ ___ then you're down. ___

ISN'T SHE LOVELY

CLARINET

Words and Music by
STEVIE WONDER

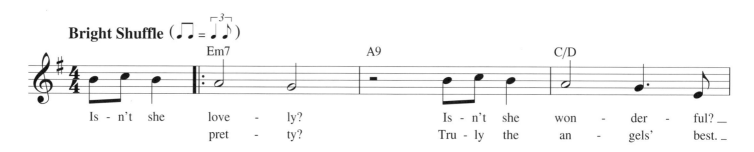

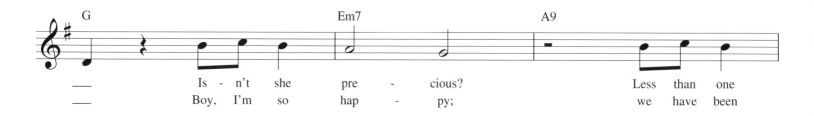

THE LETTER

CLARINET

Words and Music by
WAYNE CARSON THOMPSON

Moderately

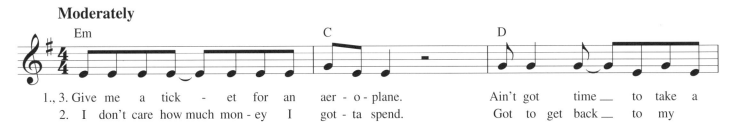

1., 3. Give me a tick - et for an aer - o - plane. Ain't got time __ to take a
2. I don't care how much mon - ey I got - ta spend. Got to get back __ to my

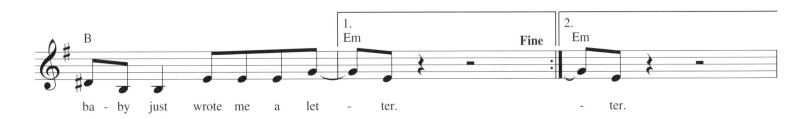

fast __ train.⎱ Lone - ly days are gone; __ I'm a - go - in' home. __ Oh, my
ba - by again.⎰

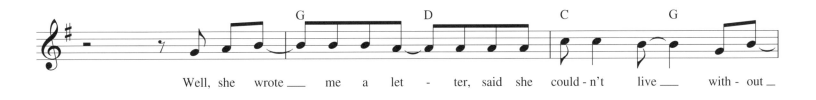

ba - by just wrote me a let - ter. - ter.

Well, she wrote __ me a let - ter, said she could - n't live __ with - out __

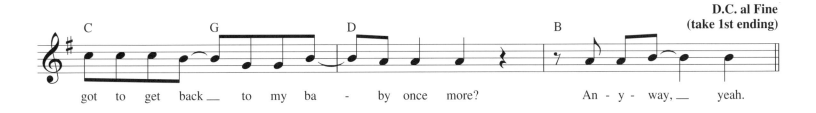

__ me no more. Lis - ten, mis - ter, can't you see I

D.C. al Fine
(take 1st ending)

got to get back __ to my ba - by once more? An - y - way, __ yeah.

LIKE A VIRGIN

CLARINET

Words and Music by BILLY STEINBERG
and TOM KELLY

THE LOOK OF LOVE

from CASINO ROYALE

CLARINET

Words by HAL DAVID
Music by BURT BACHARACH

LOVE ME TENDER

CLARINET

Words and Music by ELVIS PRESLEY
and VERA MATSON

Love me ten - der, love me sweet; nev - er let me
Love me ten - der, love me long; take me to your

go. You have made my life com - plete,
heart. For it's there my that I be - long,

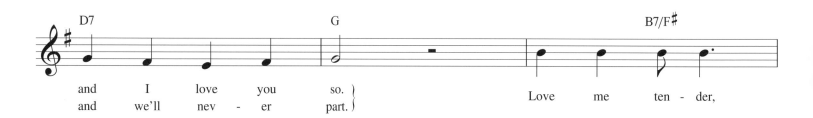

and I love you so. ⎫ Love me ten - der,
and we'll nev - er part. ⎭

love me true. All my dreams ful - fill.

For, my dar - ling, I love you, and I al - ways

will. and I al - ways will.

MR. TAMBOURINE MAN

Clarinet

Words and Music by
BOB DYLAN

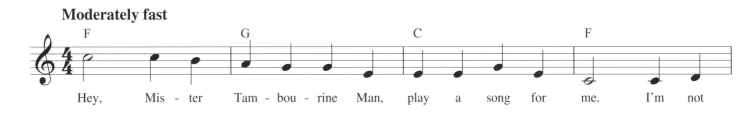

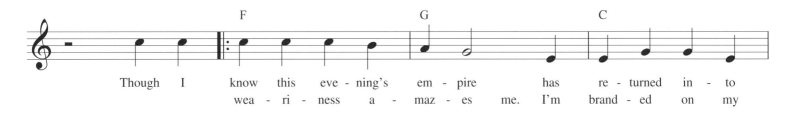

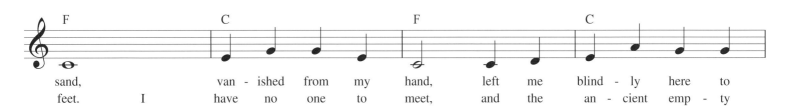

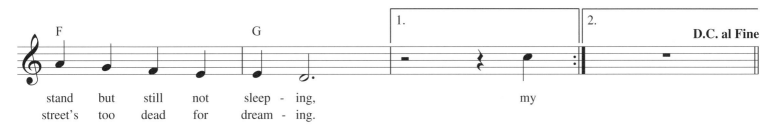

LOVE STORY

CLARINET

Words and Music by
TAYLOR SWIFT

We were both young when I first saw ___ you. I close my eyes ___ and the

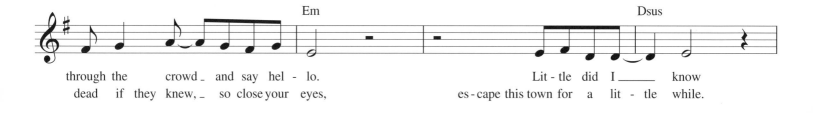

flash-back starts. _ I'm stand-ing there on a bal-co-ny in sum-mer air.

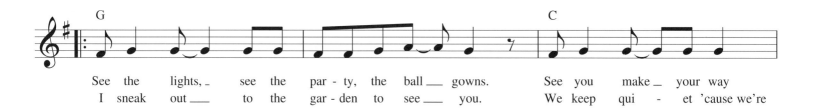

See the lights, _ see the par-ty, the ball ___ gowns. See you make ___ your way
I sneak out ___ to the gar-den to see ___ you. We keep qui - et 'cause we're

through the crowd_ and say hel - lo. Lit - tle did I _____ know
dead if they knew, _ so close your eyes, es - cape this town for a lit - tle while.

that you were Ro - me - o. You were throw-ing peb - bles, and my
'Cause you were Ro - me - o; I was the scar - let let - ter. And my

dad - dy said, "Stay a - way from Ju - li - et." ___ And I was cry - ing on the stair - case,
dad - dy said, "Stay a - way from Ju - li - et." ___ But you were ev - 'ry-thing to me. I was

beg - ging you, please,_ don't go. _____ And I ____ said:

Ro - me - o, take me some-where we can be a - lone. I'll be wait - ing.

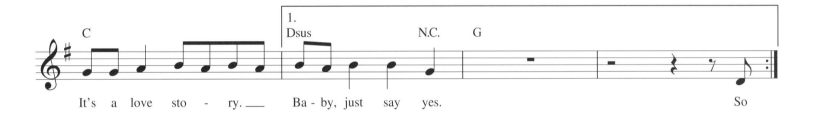

All there's left to do is run. You'll be the prince and I'll be the prin - cess.

It's a love sto - ry. ___ Ba - by, just say yes. So

Ba - by, just say ___ yes. Oh, ___ oh, oh. ___

Oh, ___ oh, oh, _____ oh.

'Cause we were both young when I first saw ___ you. ___

MOON RIVER

from the Paramount Picture BREAKFAST AT TIFFANY'S

Clarinet

Words by JOHNNY MERCER
Music by HENRY MANCINI

MORNING HAS BROKEN

Clarinet

Words by ELEANOR FARJEON
Music by CAT STEVENS

MY CHERIE AMOUR

Clarinet

Words and Music by STEVIE WONDER,
SYLVIA MOY and HENRY COSBY

MY GIRL

CLARINET

Words and Music by WILLIAM "SMOKEY" ROBINSON
and RONALD WHITE

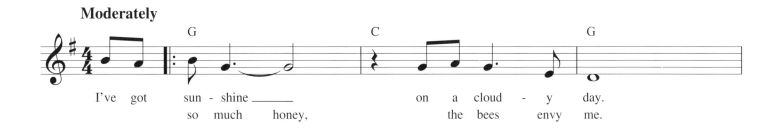

I've got sun - shine _____ on a cloud - y day.
so much honey, the bees envy me.

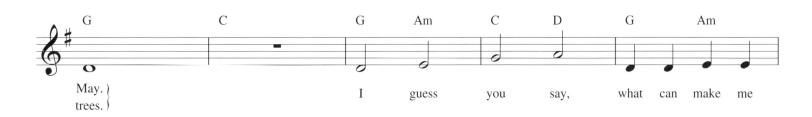

When it's cold out - side, I've got the month of
I've got a sweet - er song than the birds in the

May.
trees.
I guess you say, what can make me

feel this way? My girl. (My girl, my girl.) Talk - in' 'bout

my girl. _____ (My girl.) I've got (My girl.)

MY FAVORITE THINGS
from THE SOUND OF MUSIC

Clarinet

Lyrics by OSCAR HAMMERSTEIN II
Music by RICHARD RODGERS

Brightly

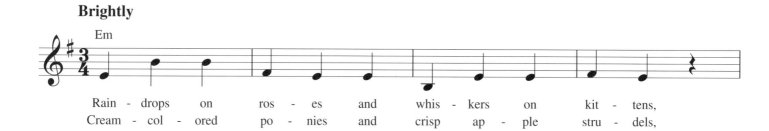

Rain - drops on ros - es and whis - kers on kit - tens,
Cream - col - ored po - nies and crisp ap - ple stru - dels,

bright cop - per ket - tles and warm wool - en mit - tens,
door - bells and sleigh - bells and schnit - zel with noo - dles,

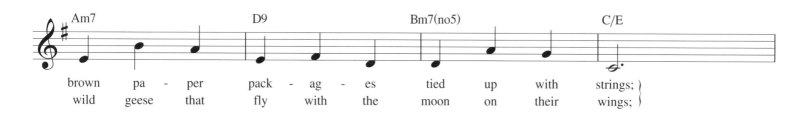

brown pa - per pack - ag - es tied up with strings;
wild geese that fly with the moon on their wings;

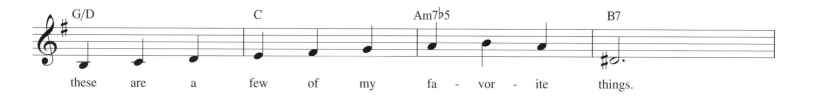

these are a few of my fa - vor - ite things.

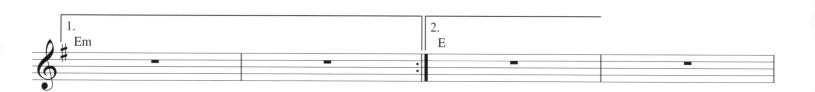

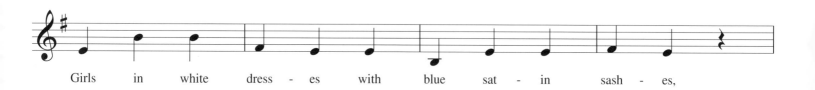

Girls in white dress - es with blue sat - in sash - es,

MY HEART WILL GO ON

(Love Theme from 'Titanic')

from the Paramount and Twentieth Century Fox Motion Picture TITANIC

CLARINET

Music by JAMES HORNER
Lyric by WILL JENNINGS

NIGHTS IN WHITE SATIN

Clarinet

Words and Music by
JUSTIN HAYWARD

NOWHERE MAN

CLARINET

Words and Music by JOHN LENNON
and PAUL McCARTNEY

PUFF THE MAGIC DRAGON

CLARINET

Words and Music by LENNY LIPTON
and PETER YARROW

RAINDROPS KEEP FALLIN' ON MY HEAD
from BUTCH CASSIDY AND THE SUNDANCE KID

CLARINET

Lyric by HAL DAVID
Music by BURT BACHARACH

SCARBOROUGH FAIR/CANTICLE

CLARINET

Arrangement and Original Counter Melody by PAUL SIMON
and ARTHUR GARFUNKEL

SOMEWHERE OUT THERE
from AN AMERICAN TAIL

Clarinet

Music by BARRY MANN and JAMES HORNER
Lyric by CYNTHIA WEIL

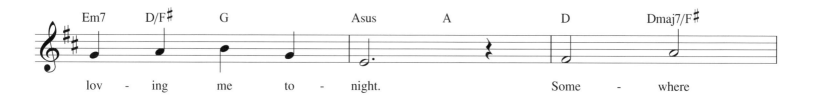

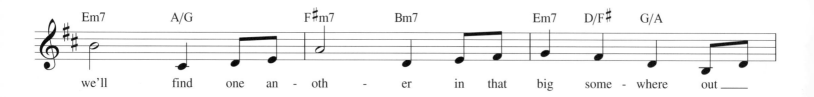

there. And e - ven though I know how ver - y far a - part we are, it

helps to think we might be wish - ing on the same bright star. And

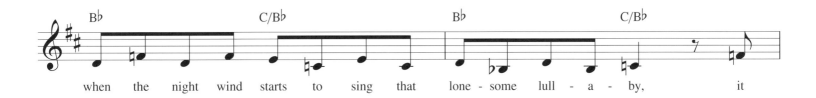

when the night wind starts to sing that lone - some lull - a - by, it

helps to think we're sleep - ing un - der - neath the same big sky.

Some - where out there, if love can see us

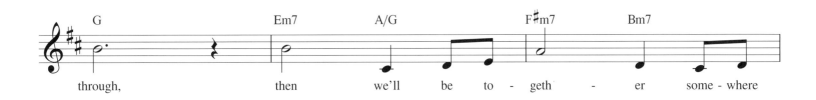

through, then we'll be to - geth - er some - where

out there, out where dreams come true.

THE SOUND OF MUSIC

from THE SOUND OF MUSIC

Clarinet

Lyrics by OSCAR HAMMERSTEIN II
Music by RICHARD RODGERS

Moderately

The hills are a - live with the sound of mu - sic, _____ with

songs they have sung for a thou - sand years. _____ The

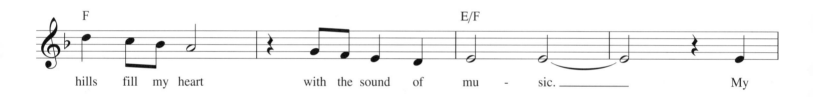

hills fill my heart with the sound of mu - sic. _____ My

heart wants to sing ev - 'ry song it hears. _____ My heart wants to

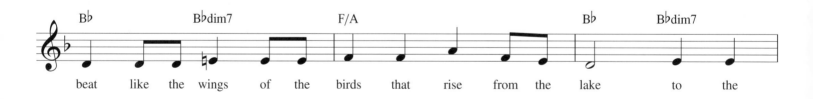

beat like the wings of the birds that rise from the lake to the

trees. My heart wants to sigh like a chime that flies from a

47

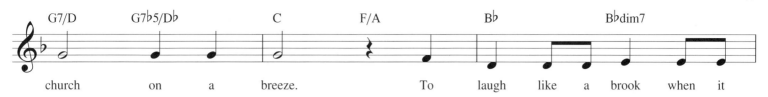

church   on   a   breeze.   To   laugh   like   a   brook   when   it

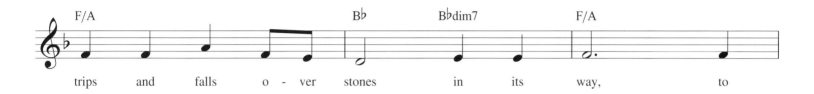

trips   and   falls   o - ver   stones   in   its   way,   to

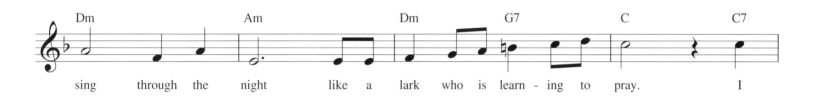

sing   through   the   night   like   a   lark   who   is   learn - ing   to   pray.   I

go   to   the   hills   when   my   heart   is   lone - ly. _____   I

know   I   will   hear   what I've heard   be - fore. _____   My

heart   will   be blessed   with   the   sound   of   mu - sic, _____   and   I'll

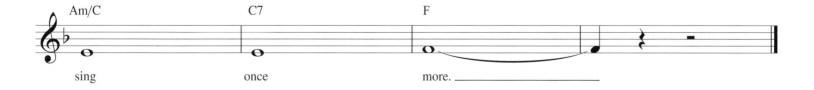

sing   once   more. _____

STRANGERS IN THE NIGHT
adapted from A MAN COULD GET KILLED

Clarinet

Words by CHARLES SINGLETON and EDDIE SNYDER
Music by BERT KAEMPFERT

SUNSHINE ON MY SHOULDERS

Clarinet

Words by JOHN DENVER
Music by JOHN DENVER, MIKE TAYLOR
and DICK KNISS

SWEET CAROLINE

Clarinet

Words and Music by
NEIL DIAMOND

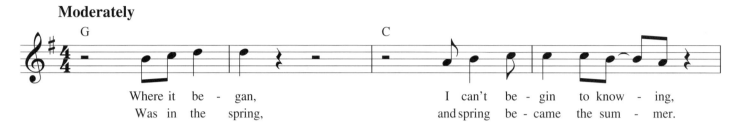

Where it be - gan, I can't be - gin to know - ing,
Was in the spring, and spring be - came the sum - mer.

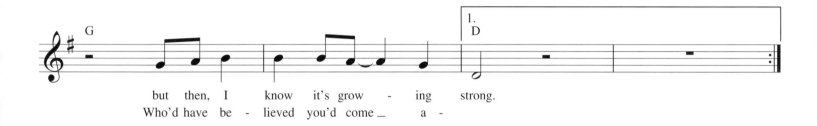

but then, I know it's grow - ing strong.
Who'd have be - lieved you'd come __ a -

long. Hands, _____ touch-ing hands, _____

reach-ing out, touch-ing me, touch-ing you. _____

Sweet Car - o - line, ___ good times nev - er seemed so
I've been in - clined ___ to be - lieve they nev - er

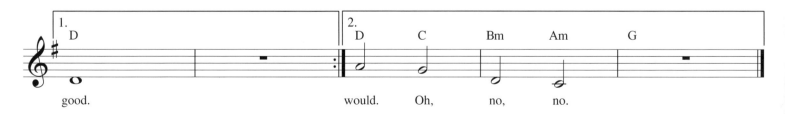

good. would. Oh, no, no.

TILL THERE WAS YOU
from Meredith Willson's THE MUSIC MAN

Clarinet

By MEREDITH WILLSON

THE TIMES THEY ARE A-CHANGIN'

CLARINET

Words and Music by
BOB DYLAN

UNCHAINED MELODY

Clarinet

Lyric by HY ZARET
Music by ALEX NORTH

TOMORROW
from The Musical Production ANNIE

CLARINET

Lyric by MARTIN CHARNIN
Music by CHARLES STROUSE

Moderately fast

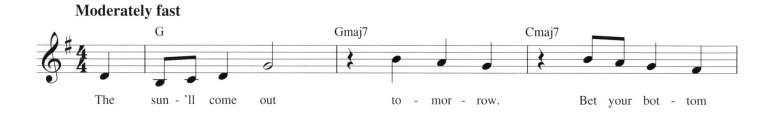

The sun - 'll come out to - mor - row. Bet your bot - tom

dol - lar that to - mor - row there'll be sun.

Just think - ing a - bout to - mor - row clears a - way the

cob - webs and the sor - row till there's none.

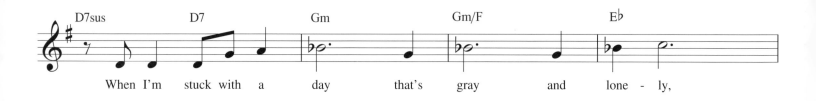

When I'm stuck with a day that's gray and lone - ly,

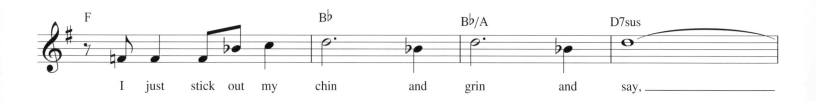

I just stick out my chin and grin and say,

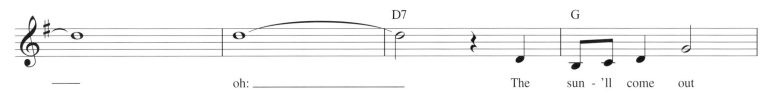

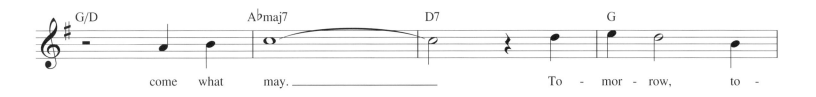

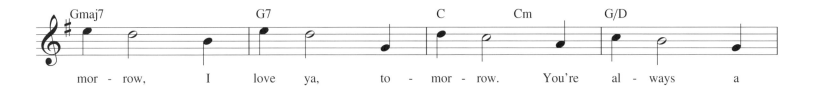

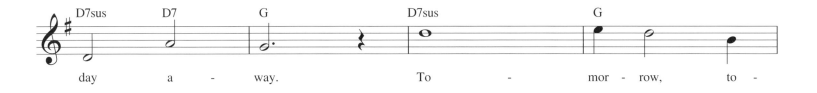

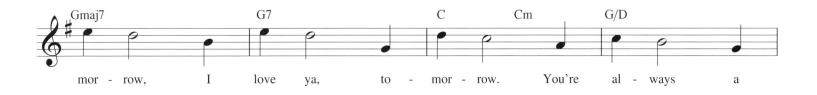

VIVA LA VIDA

Clarinet

Words and Music by GUY BERRYMAN,
JON BUCKLAND, WILL CHAMPION
and CHRIS MARTIN

me. And I dis - cov - ered that my cas - tles stand _____ up - on

pil - lars of salt _____ and pil - lars of sand. _____ I hear Je - ru - sa - lem bells _

_____ a - ring - ing. Ro - man cav - al - ry choirs ___ are sing - ing.

Be my mir - ror, my sword ___ and shield, _____ my mis - sion - ar - ies in a for -

- eign field. _____ For some rea - son I can't ___ ex - plain, __

once you've gone there was nev - er, nev - er an hon - est word, _

_____ and that was when I ruled the world. ___

WE ARE THE WORLD

CLARINET

Words and Music by LIONEL RICHIE
and MICHAEL JACKSON

WHAT A WONDERFUL WORLD

Clarinet

Words and Music by GEORGE DAVID WEISS
and BOB THIELE

WONDERWALL

CLARINET

Words and Music by
NOEL GALLAGHER

Moderately fast

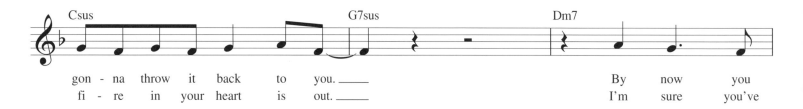

To - day is gon - na be the day that they're
Back - beat, is the word was on the street that the

gon - na throw it back to you. _____ By now you
fi - re in your heart is out. _____ I'm sure you've

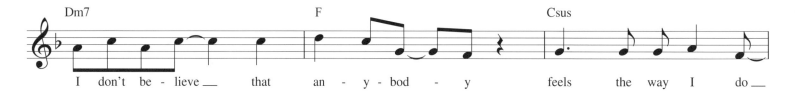

should -'ve some - how re - al - ized what you got - ta do. _____
heard it all be - fore, but you never real - ly had a doubt. ___

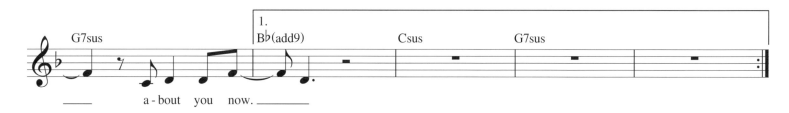

I don't be - lieve _____ that an - y - bod - y feels the way I do

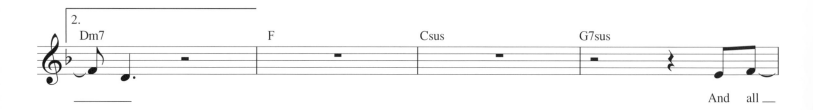

_____ a - bout you now. _____

And all _____

_____ the roads _____ we have _____ to walk _____ are wind - ing, and all _____

_____ the lights _ that lead _____ us there _ are blind - ing.

There are man - y things _____ that I _____ would like to say to you, _

_____ but I don't know how. _____

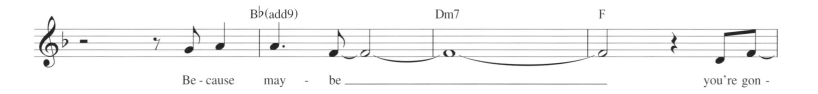

Be - cause may - be _____ you're gon -

- na be the one that saves me, _____ and

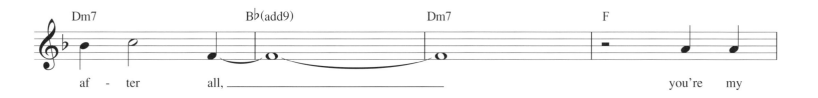

af - ter all, _____ you're my

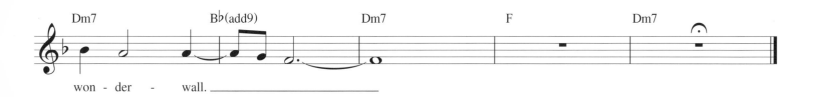

won - der - wall. _____

YOU ARE THE SUNSHINE OF MY LIFE

Clarinet

Words and Music by
STEVIE WONDER

You are the sun - shine of ___ my life. ___
You are the ap - ple of ___ my eye. ___

That's why I'll al - ways be ___ a - round. ___
For - ev - er you'll ___ stay in ___ my heart. ___

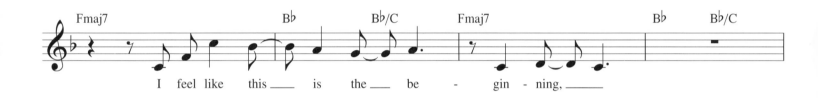

I feel like this ___ is the ___ be - gin - ning, ___

though I've loved you ___ for a thou - sand years. ___

And if I thought ___ our love ___ was end - ing, ___ I'd find ___

D.C. al Fine
(take repeat)

___ my - self ___ drown - ing in my ___ own tears. Whoa, ___ whoa. ___

YOU'VE GOT A FRIEND

CLARINET

Words and Music by
CAROLE KING

HAL•LEONARD
EASY INSTRUMENTAL PLAY-ALONG

Audio Access Included

- Perfect for beginning players
- Carefully edited to include only the notes and rhythms that students learn in the first months playing their instrument
- Great-sounding demonstration and play-along tracks
- Audio tracks can be accessed online for download or streaming, using the unique code inside the book

DISNEY
Book with Online Audio Tracks

The Ballad of Davy Crockett • Can You Feel the Love Tonight • Candle on the Water • I Just Can't Wait to Be King • The Medallion Calls • Mickey Mouse March • Part of Your World • Whistle While You Work • You Can Fly! You Can Fly! You Can Fly! • You'll Be in My Heart (Pop Version).

00122184	Flute	$9.99
00122185	Clarinet	$9.99
00122186	Alto Sax	$9.99
00122187	Tenor Sax	$9.99
00122188	Trumpet	$9.99
00122189	Horn	$9.99
00122190	Trombone	$9.99
00122191	Violin	$9.99
00122192	Viola	$9.99
00122193	Cello	$9.99
00122194	Keyboard Percussion	$9.99

CLASSIC ROCK
Book with Online Audio Tracks

Another One Bites the Dust • Born to Be Wild • Brown Eyed Girl • Dust in the Wind • Every Breath You Take • Fly like an Eagle • I Heard It Through the Grapevine • I Shot the Sheriff • Oye Como Va • Up Around the Bend.

00122195	Flute	$9.99
00122196	Clarinet	$9.99
00122197	Alto Sax	$9.99
00122198	Tenor Sax	$9.99
00122201	Trumpet	$9.99
00122202	Horn	$9.99
00122203	Trombone	$9.99
00122205	Violin	$9.99
00122206	Viola	$9.99
00122207	Cello	$9.99
00122208	Keyboard Percussion	$9.99

CLASSICAL THEMES
Book with Online Audio Tracks

Can Can • Carnival of Venice • Finlandia • Largo from Symphony No. 9 ("New World") • Morning • Musette in D Major • Ode to Joy • Spring • Symphony No. 1 in C Minor, Fourth Movement Excerpt • Trumpet Voluntary.

00123108	Flute	$9.99
00123109	Clarinet	$9.99
00123110	Alto Sax	$9.99
00123111	Tenor Sax	$9.99
00123112	Trumpet	$9.99
00123113	Horn	$9.99
00123114	Trombone	$9.99
00123115	Violin	$9.99
00123116	Viola	$9.99
00123117	Cello	$9.99
00123118	Keyboard Percussion	$9.99

CHRISTMAS CAROLS
Book with Online Audio Tracks

Angels We Have Heard on High • Christ Was Born on Christmas Day • Come, All Ye Shepherds • Come, Thou Long-Expected Jesus • Good Christian Men, Rejoice • Jingle Bells • Jolly Old St. Nicholas • Lo, How a Rose E'er Blooming • On Christmas Night • Up on the Housetop.

00130363	Flute	$9.99
00130364	Clarinet	$9.99
00130365	Alto Sax	$9.99
00130366	Tenor Sax	$9.99
00130367	Trumpet	$9.99
00130368	Horn	$9.99
00130369	Trombone	$9.99
00130370	Violin	$9.99
00130371	Viola	$9.99
00130372	Cello	$9.99
00130373	Keyboard Percussion	$9.99

POP FAVORITES
Book with Online Audio Tracks

Achy Breaky Heart (Don't Tell My Heart) • I'm a Believer • Imagine • Jailhouse Rock • La Bamba • Louie, Louie • Ob-La-Di, Ob-La-Da • Splish Splash • Stand by Me • Yellow Submarine.

00232231	Flute	$9.99
00232232	Clarinet	$9.99
00232233	Alto Sax	$9.99
00232234	Tenor Sax	$9.99
00232235	Trumpet	$9.99
00232236	Horn	$9.99
00232237	Trombone	$9.99
00232238	Violin	$9.99
00232239	Viola	$9.99
00232240	Cello	$9.99
00233296	Keyboard Percussion	$9.99

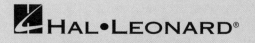

HAL•LEONARD®
www.halleonard.com

Prices, content, and availability subject to change without notice.

0917